EAST GERMAN STEAM IN THE 1970S

George Woods

AMBERLEY

First published 2017

Amberley Publishing
The Hill, Stroud
Gloucestershire, GL5 4EP

www.amberley-books.com

Copyright © George Woods, 2017

The right of George Woods to be identified as
the Author of this work has been asserted in
accordance with the Copyright, Designs and
Patents Act 1988.

ISBN 978 1 4456 7133 8 (print)
ISBN 978 1 4456 7134 5 (ebook)

British Library Cataloguing in Publication Data.
A catalogue record for this book is available from
the British Library.

Origination by Amberley Publishing.
Printed in the UK.

Introduction

During the 1970s, newspapers and television news frequently carried reports about aircraft or train enthusiasts being arrested for taking notes and photographs while pursuing their hobbies in East European countries such as Yugoslavia, Hungary and Bulgaria. They were usually released after negotiations between the various diplomatic ministries, and they returned home after spending a few days being interrogated by the secret police and having had their notebooks and film confiscated.

This was very frustrating, as behind the Iron Curtain the communist countries were still running a lot of steam locos, many of which were unusual types that were not seen in the West, or were of types that had long been taken out of service in Western Europe.

Well before the Second World War, German locomotive practice was a big influence on many East European railways, and German manufacturers such as Borsig, Henschel and Maffei supplied locos to many railways, but the most interesting types were often those designed and built locally, such as the locos developed in Austria by Karl Gölsdorf, which were spread through the countries that had come under the influence of the Austro-Hungarian Empire.

Many East European railways had received locos as war repatriations from Germany at the end of both the First and Second World Wars. These included the Class 52 Kreigsloks (war locomotives), which were built in 1942–44 in huge numbers (something like 6,750) in many of the Axis-controlled countries, often by forced labour for service on the Eastern Front. As late as the 1970s these could still be found working in Russia, Turkey, and many East European countries, and to a lesser extent in Western Europe, with many lasting until the end of steam traction, which on most railways took place in the 1970s, but didn't take place in Poland until 1993.

Several locomotive societies ran trips to Eastern Europe with varying degrees of success. It was very difficult to get a trip organised; often the railway authorities agreed to let enthusiasts have access to their stations and loco depots, and to take pictures, but because of the Cold War the security and police departments were not at all keen to allow foreigners in to take photographs, especially as transport was considered to be on the secret list, and details were not to be made available to visitors from the West.

I was a member of the Locomotive Club of Great Britain (LCGB), and when they advertised a trip to East Germany in the spring of 1975 I decided it was the best way to see East European steam, as to travel independently was very risky. I had been to West Germany several times and steam there was coming to an end, but in East Germany – or to give it its official title, the Deutsche Demokratische Republik (DDR)– plenty of steam was still to be seen in service on all types of traffic, from InterCity Expresses to slow freight traffic.

The tour itself went extremely well. For the most part we were able to photograph quite freely, and no one got arrested during the tour. The only downside was the weather, which struggled to get above freezing for most of the time.

Compared to countries in the West, everything seemed to be run down; the towns and cities were drab and could have done with a good clean and a coat of paint, and everyday necessities were in short supply. The Deutsche Reichsbahn (DR) rail system also seemed shabby and much rolling stock was elderly, with some even dating back to pre-war days still being in service.

My second trip was with To Europe for Steam, a group headed by Bill Alborough, who organised tours to see steam locos in many parts of the world. This tour took place in July 1976, which meant the weather was better – in fact, the temperature reached over 100 °F while we were in Berlin. This trip also went extremely well, although we were kept waiting for about three hours on the wrong side of the border for our guide and the tour bus after we had entered the DDR through Checkpoint Charlie in Berlin, and it was gone 3 a.m. before we got to our hotel.

After the Second World War ended, large sections of the electrified railway system in East Germany were stripped of equipment, which was transported to Russia to be used on their rail system, and many locomotives and other items were also sent to various countries in both East and West Europe as war repatriations, which left the railways in both parts of Germany with a serious shortage of equipment that was not overcome until many years later, when industry regained something like normal output. Diesel locos were gradually appearing in quite large numbers, especially two types that were manufactured in the Soviet Union, which were coming into service in most of the Eastern Bloc countries.

The lack of finance and pressure to improve other parts of the economy helped to ensure that standard-gauge steam locomotives survived on the DR until 1988, lasting much longer than in countries in the West. The UK finished with steam in 1968, while in West Germany it lasted until 1977, and in France the last of steam was retired in 1974.

The steam survivors were, in many cases, the same types that had been running in West Germany until the end of steam there, but in the DDR some types such as the Prussian G12 Class survived for much longer, with many of that type being modernised by the DR in the late 1950s. Other types, such as the Class 52 Kreigsloks, built by the Nazis during the Second World War, and the original 01 Pacifics were still in front-line service, whereas they had been withdrawn from service in West Germany some years previously.

Another big difference from Western countries was the amount of steam-worked narrow-gauge lines that survived in the DDR; many lasting until reunification in 1989. In fact, many are still running today, but either as privately owned railways or heritage railways.

The narrow-gauge lines were a highlight of both tours as each one we travelled on were worked by different types of loco and ran through different parts of the country, varying from the industrial line that ran from Oschatz to Mügeln to the system that ran through the picturesque scenery of the Harz Mountains from Nordhausen to Wernigerode. However, the most scenic line was to the Brocken, which ran very close to the border with West Germany, and as such was barred to foreign visitors.

The stars of the show on the DR were the coal-fired 01 Pacifics, which were built in the 1920s and remained largely in original condition. The last survivors were still working expresses between Berlin and Dresden, which, by this time (1975), was the last European InterCity service to be worked by steam.

Many other passenger services were worked by 01.5 Pacifics, which were rebuilt from the original 01 Class between 1962 and 1965. Most of them were equipped with oil-burning equipment, although some continued as coal burners. These locos could be seen in West Germany as they were used on cross-border services with passenger trains from Berlin and Dresden to Hamburg Altona and Bebra until the mid-1970s.

Other Eastern Bloc locos could be seen working into the DDR at various locations. We saw Czechoslovakian steam locos at Zittau, and Polish steam and diesel locos at Görlitz.

I think it is fair to say that watching and photographing trains in East Germany was almost as free and easy as in West Germany. This was probably because a lot of the locals were rail enthusiasts and so we shared a hobby, and model railways were also popular in the DDR, whereas there was not the same level of interest in railways in countries such as Bulgaria and Yugoslavia, which made the authorities all the more suspicious. Having said that, we went with a group and had permission to take pictures and visit rail installations. Things could have been a lot different if we had tried to do these things by ourselves or in a small group – that is, if we could get an entry visa in the first place.

I made further trips to Poland and Czechoslovakia soon after with the LCGB, and although we did well on the whole for taking pictures, we did so with quite a few restrictions.

How things have changed since the fall of the Berlin Wall in 1989, and the reunification of Germany in 1990. I sat in front of the television as the news came in, and could not believe what was happening as East Germans crossed the border into West Berlin without resistance, and Checkpoint Charlie, where we had had to wait so long in 1976, was now just part of history. Soviet influence had seemed so impregnable that it was hard to imagine how any changes would take place without major conflict. Now tourism to Russia and nearly all of the East European countries is accepted as normal. If only it had been like that back in the 1960s and '70s; it is frustrating to think of all the opportunities that were missed because of the restrictive regimes, but we must be thankful that at least we were able to see some of what Eastern European railways had to offer.

George Woods, 2017

Abbreviations

Bf	Bahnhof – Railway Station
BMAG	Berliner Maschinenbau
Bw	Bahnbetriebswerk – Locomotive Depot
DB	Deutsche Bundesbahn – West German Railways
DR	Deutsche Reichsbahn – East German Railways
DDR	Deutsche Demokratische Republik – German Democratic Republic
Hbf	Hauptbahnhof – Main or Central Station
O&K	Orenstein & Koppel
VEB	Volkseigener Betrieb

The following four pictures were taken on the 900 mm gauge line, nicknamed the Molli, which runs the 15.4 kilometres from Bad Doberan to Kühlungsborn West on the Baltic Coast. The three 2-8-2T locos that work the line were built in 1932 by O&K. The line remains open today with the same locos and rolling stock still in service. Pictures were taken on 30 May 1975.

Narrow Gauge

No. 99 2322 has just arrived at Bad Doberan with the 13.11 from Ostseebad Kühlungsborn West.

No. 99 2323 waits at Bad Doberan for its next train. The first part of the line runs down the main street of Bad Doberan and then follows the main road to Kühlungsborn.

Above and below: No. 99 2323 waits for departure at Ostseebad Kühlungsborn West with the 14.15 train to Bad Doberan. This Baltic Sea resort is very popular in the summer months.

The following five pictures were taken on the 750 mm gauge line that runs from Putbus to Göhren on the island of Rugen, which is on the Baltic Sea coast. The line is still open to traffic today. Pictures taken 31 March 1975.

Above and below: No. 99 4801 2-8-0T, built by Henschel in 1938, calls at Binz Ost with the 10.26 Putbus to Göhren train.

No. 99 4801 at Binz Ost with the 12.00 Göhren to Putbus train.

No. 99 4802 2-8-0T, built by Henschel in 1938, is seen dumped at Putbus Bw but will be restored to service.

No. 99 4644 0-8-0T, built by O&K in 1923, is also stored out of service at Putbus Bw and will also be preserved.

The following seven pictures were taken on the 16.1 km-long 750 mm gauge Zittau to Kurort Oybin and Kurort Jonsdorf system. The line remains open and is still steam worked. Pictures taken on 2 April 1975.

No. 99 4532 0-8-0T, built by O&K in 1924, was specially moved to Zittau station so that we could get photos.

No. 99 1757 2-10-2T, built by BMAG in 1933, seen at Zittau Hbf with the 13.26 departure to Kurort Jonsdorf.

No. 99 1757 calls at Zittau Süd.

The scene at Bertsdorf, with No. 99 1757 on the left with the 14.03 to Kurort Jonsdorf, and No. 99 1746 (built by BMAG in 1929) waiting on the right with the 14.04 to Kurort Oybin. Both trains usually made a simultaneous departure for photographers.

The crew of No. 99 1757 pose for their picture with the station mistress at Bertsdorf.

Above and below: No. 99 1759, built by BMAG in 1933, poses for the camera at Kurort Oybin before running round its train for the journey back to Bertsdorf and Zittau.

The following four pictures were taken on 3 April 1975 at the Radebeul Ost depot, which serves the 16.5 km-long 750 mm gauge line to Radeburg. The line remains open and is still steam worked.

No. 99 715 0-10-0T, built by Hartman in 1927, is a standby loco that has been preserved and remains in service today.

No. 99 1786 2-10-2T, built by O&K in 1954, is being coaled and watered in readiness for its day's work.

Above and below: No. 99 1793, built by O&K in 1956, is outside the shed for repair, and No. 99 1786 is ready to work its next train.

The following five pictures were taken on the 11.4 km-long 750 mm gauge line from Oschatz to Mügeln on 3 April 1975. The line, which became freight only in 1993, closed its freight services in 2001, but still runs some school trains and special steam-hauled services.

At Oschatz, No. 99 1562 0-4-4-0, built by Hartman in 1909, on the left, has a train of transporter wagons loaded with standard-gauge wagons, and on the right No. 99 1563 has a mixed train of passenger and freight stock.

No. 99 1562 stands in the yard at Oschatz as Russian soldiers unload a coal wagon by hand in the background!

No. 99 1564, built by Hartman in 1909, runs up the yard at Oschatz with a van, which it will attach to the mixed train.

A very well looked-after No. 99 1562 poses in the sun at Oschatz. Ninety-six of these Meyer articulated locos were built by the Saxon Railways between 1892 and 1921.

At the other end of the line, No. 99 1563, built by Hartman in 1909, stands outside the shed at Mügeln.

The following fourteen pictures were taken on the 21.9 km metre gauge Gernrode (Harz) to Strassberg (Harz) system, known as the Selketalbahn, which is still open for traffic. Pictures taken on 18 July 1976.

No. 99 5901 0-4-4-0, built by Jung in 1897, arrives at Strassberg with the one-coach train from Gernrode.

No. 99 5902 0-4-4-0, built by Jung in 1897, arrives at Alexisbad with a train from Gernrode.

No. 99 5901 attracts many admirers at Strassberg while waiting to leave with the 12.55 departure to Alexisbad.

No. 99 5901 runs round
its train at Alexisbad and
departs for the short journey
to Harzgerode.

No. 99 5902 and No. 5901 wait at Alexisbad with their trains for Strassberg and Gernrode.

Above and below: At Mägdesprung, we passed No. 99 6001 2-6-2T, which was built by Krupp in 1939, with a train headed for Alexisbad.

No. 99 5901 stands at Gernrode (Harz) with our train from Gernrode.

The following six pictures were taken on the metre gauge line from Nordhausen to Wernigerode, known as the Harzquerbahn, which uses large 2-10-2T locos built in 1954–56 by VEB (formerly O&K). Still steam worked, the line remains open to traffic. Pictures taken on 19 July 1976.

Above and below: No. 99 7247 2-10-2 waits at Nordhausen Nord with the 10.06 departure for Wernigerode.

Above and below: At Eisfelder Talmühle we passed a train heading for Nordhausen.

No. 99 7247 takes water at Eisfelder Talmühle.

No. 99 7247 awaits departure at Benneckesteine.

The following ten pictures were taken on the 750 mm gauge line from Wolkenstein to Jöhstadt on 21 July 1976. Known as the Pressnitztalbahn, the line was closed in 1986, but the section from Jöhstadt to Steinbach has been reopened as a heritage line.

No. 99 1586 0-4-4-0, built by Hartman in 1913, is being prepared for our train at Wolkenstein MPD.

On a wet morning, No. 99 1586 waits to depart from Wolkenstein with the 09.36 to Jöhstadt.

No. 99 1586 *Niederschmiedeberg* stops at Streckwalde, but there are no passengers today.

No. 99 1586 *Niederschmiedeberg* looks like it might have passengers but it was only our group on the platform taking pictures.

No. 99 1586 sees real passengers leaving the train at Oberschmiedeberg.

Above and below: No. 99 1586 takes water at Steinbach bei Jöhstadt.

No. 99 1586 performs a run past for the cameras at Schmalzgrube.

No. 99 1586 has just arrived at Jöhstadt and has some passengers for the return journey.

No. 99 1594, built by Hartman in 1913, and No. 99 1583, built by Hartman in 1912, are in store at the small shed at Jöhstadt.

The following four pictures were taken on 21 July 1976 on the 17.3 km 750 mm gauge line from Cranzahl to Kurort Oberwiesenthal, which runs very close to the border with the Czech Republic. The line remains open and still operates steam-hauled services.

No. 99 1791 2-10-2, built by O&K in 1956, is seen at the small loco shed at Cranzahl while waiting to be taken to the narrow-gauge works at Gorlitz for an overhaul.

No. 99 1782, built by O&K in 1953, and its crew pass the time while waiting to depart from Cranzahl with the 13.48 to Kurort Oberwiesenthal.

No. 99 1782 calls at Neudorf.

No. 99 1771, built by O&K in 1953, waits at Kurort Oberwiesenthal with the 16.23 to Cranzahl. It is very busy here in the winter as it is a popular centre for winter sports, and at 892 metres is the highest town in Germany.

The following few pictures of East German Class 01.5 Pacifics, which used to work cross-border services on a daily basis, were taken in West Germany at Hamburg, Buchen and Bebra.

No. 01 0527 4-6-2 has just arrived at Hamburg Altona on 3 September 1972 with a train from Dresden.

No. 01 0509 4-6-2 waits to leave Hamburg Hbf with the 09.00 to Dresden on 4 September 1972. No. 01 0509 has been preserved and is currently at Espenhain.

No. 01 0509 departs from Buchen with the 09.36 to Dresden on 4 September 1972.

At Hamburg Altona Hbf on 4 September 1972, West German No. 01 2071 (DB) 4-6-2 has arrived on a train from Westerland, and is waiting to back out to the loco sheds for servicing. Below, No. 01 0527 waits to depart with an afternoon train to Berlin.

Above and below: No. 01 0509 at Hamburg Altona on 4 September 1972 with an arrival from Dresden, which seems to consist mostly of West German coaches.

No. 01 0527 waits to depart from Hamburg Altona on 5 September 1972 with the 08.43 to Dresden.

No. 01 0523 4-6-2 waits to depart from Bebra Hbf in West Germany with the afternoon train to Frankfurt (Oder) on 5 September 1972.

No. 01 0533 4-6-2 is on the turntable at Bebra Bw on 5 September 1972.

No. 01 0533 4-6-2 departs from Bebra with an afternoon train for Dresden on 5 September 1972.

No. 01 0521 waits to depart from Magdeburg Hbf on 29 March 1975 with the 08.36 to Rostock.

No. 50 0005 2-10-0, rebuilt in 1965, is seen at Wittenberge Bw on 29 March 1975.

No. 41 1033 2-8-2, built in 1936, is seen at Wittenberge Bw on 29 March 1975.

No. 50 4022 2-10-0 was built in 1956 and is seen at Schwerin Bw on 29 March 1975.

No. 50 4043 2-10-0, built in 1960, has just arrived at Schwerin Hbf on 29 March 1975.

No. 35 1084 2-6-2, built 1955–59, was one of 113 built as Class 23.10 and is in use as a stationary boiler at Wismar Bw on 30 March 1975.

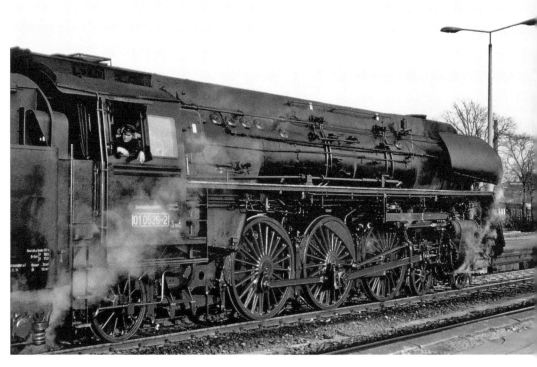

A well-polished No. 01 0526 4-6-2 waits for departure time at Stralsund Hbf on 31 March 1975 with the 17.26 to Berlin.

No. 52 6920 2-10-0 passes Berlin Schönefeld with a southbound freight on 1 April 1975.

No. 01 2207 and No. 03 2234 arrive at Berlin Schönefeld with the 12.52 to Dresden on 1 April 1975.

The following seven pictures were taken at Dresden Neustadt Hbf on 1 April 1975.

No. 52 6431 2-10-0 passes light engine.

No. 52 1042 2-10-0 calls with a local train to Dresden Hbf.

No. 52 8056 2-10-0 poses in the evening sun. No. 52 8056 has been preserved at Bautzen station.

No. 35 1061 2-6-2 departs with a local train towards Dresden.

No. 50 1851-52-6431 pass with a northbound freight.

No. 03 2214 4-6-2 calls with another local service bound for Dresden.

Above and below: No. 03 2214 backs on to and departs from Görlitz Hbf with the 11.19 to Frankfurt (Oder), which conveys through coaches from Warsaw to Paris. Görlitz is on the border with Poland and is an engine changing point for through services. Taken on 2 April 1975.

No. 52 6902 2-10-0 stands at the imposing Zittau Hbf on 2 April 1975 with a local train to Löbau.

No. 01 1515 4-6-2 passes Radebeul Ost with the 07.42 Berlin Dresden Express on 3 April 1975.

No. 35 1018 2-6-2 leaves Dresden Neustadt Hbf with a local train on 3 April 1975.

No. 50 1860 2-10-0 pauses at Dresden Neustadt Hbf with a northbound freight train on 3 April 1975.

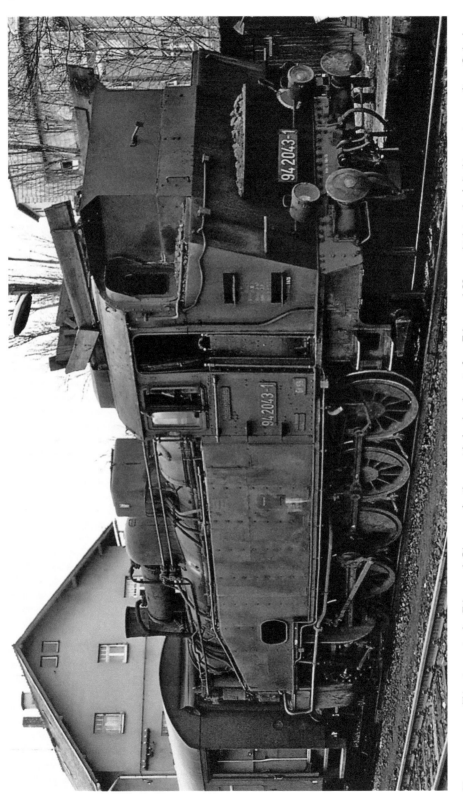

No. 94 2043 o-1o-oT has just arrived at Eibenstock Ober on 4 April 1975 with the shuttle train from Eibenstock Unter, which involved climbing a 1 in 25 gradient. Only three of these former Saxon Railways locos were in service at this time and were withdrawn from service shortly after our visit.

The following seven pictures were taken at Aue Hbf on 4 April 1975.

Above and below: No. 58 2051 2-10-0 waits to depart with a freight train for Karl Marx Stadt.

No. 86 1589 2–8–2T shunts freight wagons.

Above and below: No. 58 1562 was one of 1,478 Class G12s built between 1917 and 1924 for the Prussian State Railways and several other German railways. The last one was taken out of service by the DR in 1976.

Above and below: No. 86 1775 2-8-2 waits to depart with the 13.56 local passenger train to Schwarzenberg.

The following eight pictures were taken at Saalfeld Bw on 5 April 1975.

No. 41 1231 2-8-2 is one of 366 built between 1937 and 1941. No. 41 1231 has been preserved at Stassfurt.

No. 41 1289 2-8-2 is stored out of service. No. 41 1289 has been preserved at Falkenberg.

No. 44 0414 2-10-0. This was one of ninety-one locos converted to oil burning for the DR in 1963, but this one is stored out of use, and may be waiting to make its last journey to the scrapyard.

No. 44 0569. Nearly 2,000 of this type were constructed between 1926 and 1949, and the last one was retired in 1977.

No. 65 1020 2-8-4T. Ninety-five of these locos were built between 1954 and 1957 and the last ones ran in 1977.

No. 65 1015 2-8-4T has just arrived with a passenger train, and is being serviced for its next journey.

No. 01 0534 4-6-2. Thirty-five 01.5s were rebuilt from 01s in 1962–65, and the last one, No. 01 0519, ran in 1991.

No. 95 0020 2-10-2T. Forty-five 95 locos were built from 1922–23 to a Prussian Railways design by Borsig & Hanomag, and all were retired by 1978.

The following seven pictures were taken at Saalfeld Hbf on 5 April 1975.

Above and below: The guard of a train to Gera, gives the crew of No. 65 1073 2-8-4T details of the journey just prior to departure.

Above and below: No. 01 0501 4-6-2 receives some last-minute attention before departing with the 13.15 to Leipzig.

No. 44 0413 2-10-0 waits at the signal for permission to proceed to the shed for servicing.

No. 95 0009 2-10-2T arrives with a freight from the Leipzig direction. No. 95 0009 has been preserved at Dieringhausen Railway Museum.

No. 95 0045 2-10-2T waits to depart with the 14.24 service to Sonneberg, which consists of double-deck coaches.

No. 41 1189 2-8-2 stands on Saalfeld Bw. This photo was taken from the train as we left for Gera on 5 April 1975.

No. 58 3015 2-10-0 passes Gera Hbf light engine.

No. 44 0280 2-10-0 stands at Gera Hbf on 5 April 1975.

No. 58 3041 2-10-0 departs from the freight yard and climbs through Gera Hbf with a heavy southbound freight train on 5 April 1975.

Above and below: No. 03 2098 4-6-2 Berlin-Schöneweide Bw on a very hot 17 July 1976. The temperature was just over 100 °F. No. 03 2098 has been preserved at the Technik Museum Speyer.

No. 52 4924 2-10-0 at Berlin-Schöneweide MPD on 17 July 1976. No. 52 4924 has been preserved at the Saxon Railway Museum in Chemnitz-Hilbersdorf.

No. 03 2155 4-6-2 departs from Berlin Ost Hbf on 17 July 1976 with the 14.03 to Leipzig. No. 03 2155 has been preserved at Nossen.

No. 50 3556 2-10-0 departs from Halberstadt with the 16.30 to Dedeleben on 19 July 1976. No. 50 3556 has been preserved at Strassfurt.

No. 35 1107 2-6-2 waits to leave Karl Marx Stadt (Chemnitz) on 20 July 1976 with the 06.51 to Mittweida. At this time the station was being completely rebuilt.

The following twelve pictures were taken at Leipzig Hbf on 20 July 1976.

No. 03 2236 4-6-2 waits for departure with the 08.56 to Berlin, and then makes a very smoky departure. The station at Leipzig is one of the largest in the world, and when built had twenty-six platforms. It was badly damaged by bombing towards the end of the Second World War and train services were completely stopped for some months in 1945. It was gradually rebuilt and today is one of the finest stations in Europe.

No. 01 0501 4-6-2 arrives with a train from Saalefeld.

No. 01 0501 rests under the imposing roof after arriving at Platform 3 with the 07.12 from Saalfeld, and is waiting for the train to depart before going to the loco sheds for servicing.

No. 41 1231 2-8-2 waits to
depart with the 11.36 to
Saalfeld via Gera.

No. 01 0519 4-6-2 waits to go to the loco sheds for servicing before working its next train. No. 01 0519 has been preserved at Rottweil.

Above and below: No. 01 0501 departs with its return working to Saalfeld.

No. 86 1193 waits to depart from Thermalbad Wiesenbad on 21 July 1976 with the 18.41 train to Flöha.

No. 86 1193 2–8–2 crosses Cranzahl Viaduct with the 13.46 to Bärenstein on 21 July 1976.

No. 50 1317 2-10-0 roars up the gradient on the single line through Waldkirchen (Erzgeb) on 21 July 1976 with a freight train, heading towards Karl Marx Stadt.

The following five pictures were taken on 22 July 1976 and show trains crossing the Marien Bridge, which crosses the River Elbe in Dresden. The bridge was opened in 1852 and has recently been rebuilt to cope with modern traffic levels.

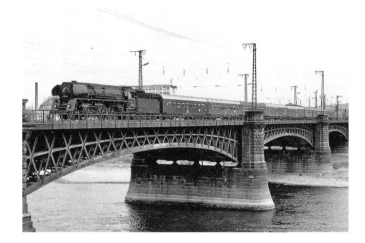

No. 01 1511 4-6-2 passes with an express for Dresden.

No. 01 2207 4-6-2 is working a Berlin to Dresden Express.

No. 01 2214 4-6-2 is heading for Berlin with an express, which includes through coaches on the rear from Budapest.

No. 50 2347-52 8047 are heading for the freight yards to pick up their trains. No. 52 8047 has been preserved at Nossen.

The following five pictures show trains passing through Dresden Mitte station, which were also taken on 22 July 1976.

No. 01 2120 4-6-2 passes with an express from Berlin. The blue coaches at the front of the train will go through to Budapest.

No. 01 2165 and No. 01 2029 are on their way to Dresden station to work express services later that afternoon.

No. 52 8193 2-10-0 gets stopped at a red signal while working a northbound freight.

No. 01 1511 4-6-2 passes Radebeul-Weintraube on 22 July 1976 with a train for Rostock.

No. 03 2100 4-6-2 departs from Dresden Neustadt on 22 July 1976 with the 15.20 to Görlitz.

No. 01 2114 4-6-2 arrives at Dresden Hbf on 22 July 1976 with an express from Berlin.

Photographed from our bedroom in the Hotel Ibis, a 52 2-10-0 leaves Dresden Hbf on 24 July 1976 with a southbound local train.

Above and below: No. 01 1511 4-6-2 backs down onto its Berlin express and waits for departure time at Dresden Hbf on 24 July 1976.

No. 01 2114 4-6-2 is waiting at Dresden Hbf on 24 July 1976 to depart for Berlin.

The following seven pictures were taken at Zwickau Bw on 24 July 1976.

Left: No. 58 3024 2-10-0 stands on the turntable leading into the roundhouse-style shed.

Below: Nos 58 3003 and 58 2129. The rebuilt No. 58 3003 is on the left, and one of the original G12s on the right.

No. 58 3047 stands on the turntable. The last 58 was retired in 1981. and No. 58 3047 has been preserved and is located in Glauchau.

Nos 58 3006 and 58 3053 stand outside the roundhouse waiting to be fired up for their next duties.

Three views of No. 58
3006 2-10-0. Fifty-six
of these powerful
three-cylinder locos were
rebuilt from the Prussian
Railways' G12s in 1958–62.

No. 86 1001 2-8-2T stands at Kwonitz with a freight train for Aue on 24 July 1976.

No. 86 1126 2-8-2T and No. 58 1246 2-10-0 are dumped at Lossnitz on 24 July 1976, waiting to be towed away for scrapping.

The following five pictures were taken at Aue Hbf on 24 July 1976.

Above and below: No. 86 1725 2-8-2T were built by many works in Germany and Austria from 1928. The last ones remained in service for only about six months after this photo was taken.

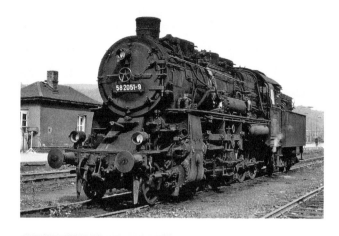

G12 No. 58 2051. These three-cylinder 2-10-0 locos were built by the Prussian Railways in 1917–21, and would only remain in service for another six months before they were all withdrawn from service.

Right and below: G12 No. 58 2100 runs through the station before it leaves Aue with a freight for the south on 24 July 1976.

The following five pictures were taken at Berlin Ostbahnhof on 25 July 1976.

Above and below: No. 01 2204 4-6-2 has just arrived from Dresden with an express.

No. 01 0527 4-6-2 waits to depart with an express.

No. 01 2120 4-6-2 arrives with a train from the south.

No. 01 2207 4-6-2 climbs out of an underpass with a southbound train as it leaves Berlin Hbf.